THIS IS ME

MATTHEW CESARIO

Cesario Publishing

Table of Contents

Acknowledgments

"Where would I be without you?"
— Admiral William H. McRaven

To my beautiful wife, Megan, my best friend, my soul-mate. What a life we have had together so far! Words can't describe how excited I am in seeing what this universe brings to us in the future; good or bad, I know we can get through anything. To my three children, Jacob, Brianna, and Kaia. I'm so proud to be your father, and I cannot wait to witness the positive changes you'll bring to this world. And to the family and friends who were there for me when I needed it the most, I thank you with all the love and gratitude I can offer. Because of you, I'm able to have the opportunity to make my dreams come true.

Introduction

"You take the red pill; you stay in Wonderland,
and I show you how deep the rabbit hole goes."
— Morpheus

The first thing I would like to say is thank you! Whether you've picked up this book because of a recommendation or maybe you found it on a table at your local dentist office or possibly it just somehow ended up in your hands by accident, regardless of the way, from the bottom of my heart, in all seriousness, thank you.

I have one main purpose in sharing my story with you. That purpose is having the opportunity to help others. I remember feeling very alone at times, feeling like nobody understood what I what going through. You see it has taken me forty years. Wait a second. I'm not going to count the ages. Let's say from birth to about well, personally, age twenty-five. And the students in the classroom raise their hands and they all say at once,

"Why age twenty-five?" Good question. My two cents only here. I'm not a licensed professional about child psychology, nor do I have a background in studying human behavioral patterns, but for me the adult responsibilities and thought process didn't start until I was twenty-five years old, and that's the age when I married my beautiful wife. So from twenty-five years of age and as I'm writing this book I'm two months away from turning forty, so it's taken me almost fifteen years into coming to this realization. P.T. Barnum once said, "The noblest art is that of making others happy," truly an amazing quote and perspective. I have learned that the noblest art is that of helping others. Now we both understand that there can be more to that on beliefs and perspectives, and I'm definitely not saying Mr. Barnum is wrong by any means. The act of helping others has transformed my life, and before my life could be transformed, it had to be saved.

I hope after reading my story, you can understand how much helping others in need has impacted my life. If you are going through similar difficulties, please know that if I can get through this, you can too. You can have hope for a better life as long as you have faith in something bigger than yourself because we can never do this alone.

CHAPTER I

You Matter, and You're Special

"I am not your rolling wheels/I am the highway/I am not your carpet ride/I am the sky/I am not your blowing wind/I am the lightning/I am not your autumn moon/I am the night."

—Audioslave

Before I get into sharing my story and journey, I would like to start off by recognizing YOU. No matter what religion or science you believe in, and what you may have been told growing up, YOU ARE SPECIAL, YOU'RE UNIQUE, and in this crazy world and endless universe, YOU MATTER. Not too long ago whenever I had heard something similar to this, I would cringe, roll my eyes, laugh, and chuckle. Basically, every thought or action was negative. I had feelings of helplessness, hopelessness, and resentment. My previous perspective was small-minded and honestly easier than putting in the work.

Can anyone relate? Have you ever had these feelings and perspectives toward yourself? Have you ever felt you don't belong, a constant, continuous feeling of being lost and alone? Have you ever gotten to the point of even contemplating ending your life?

We are "opening a can of worms" right now. An inspiration of mine, Gary V, would say, "This is real-life shit we're talking here!"

It doesn't matter if you're in elementary school, middle school, high school, or finished with school. This type of negative thought process is going on, and the longer this type of toxic perspective exists, the deeper the rabbit hole will get. I also know I'm not alone when I say that damn rabbit hole can feel dark and deep and a never-ending feeling of free falling.

Okay, now that we've identified the fears and dark times that we all experience at some point in our lives, we are going to shift our feelings, thoughts, and focus back to a positive environment and mindset. I'm not going to get into the details about why keeping a positive energy and mindset is essential, because there are professionals who specialize in this particular area. I highly recommend checking out the book *The Seat of the Soul* by Gary Zukav. This book can change your life.

What's important is to start practicing having a positive and optimistic mindset and perspective. One of the many perspectives I've learned that has helped in changing my mindset is that what we put out into the world/universe is what comes back to us. Whether that's positive or negative is up to us.

Over time, daily practice of having positive perspectives, emotions, feelings, thoughts, actions, and responses will help in one HUGE, ESSENTIAL, EPIC way: to love yourself. To love yourself know matter what anyone else thinks, says, writes about, texts about, or DM's about. To love yourself when others don't and doubt you. To love yourself when you fail at something, and to still love yourself after you fail again and again and again. To love yourself when you make mistakes. I can't tell you or emphasis enough how important this is in our lives. It is important for our growth, our happiness, and our survival.

CHAPTER 2

On This Day

"You've Been Violated!"

—Violator

On this day, my life would be changed forever. Unfortunately, it would not be for the best. After this day, fear, anger, periods or rage, depression, worthlessness, thoughts of suicide, resentment, pain, and suffering would RULE my life and those involved in it. Every single day, sometimes many moments throughout, would push me toward insanity. One of the worst parts is that I had not told anyone about this incident until I was twenty-one years of age, and she is now my wife. It wasn't until nine years ago that I shared this with someone other than my wife. I learned how to put up boundaries at the young age of eight.

When I was eight years old, I was a victim of sexual molestation. This was a single incident, thank goodness, but reasons for not saying anything still haunt me from time to time. Sometimes random things and situations will give me sudden flashbacks. Flashbacks of the dirty wet, cold cement garage floor. The smell of gasoline combined with a fowl musty odor. Flashbacks of a hand on my throat and mouth. Being whispered things as if it was coming from Lucifer himself. Flashbacks of the feeling of complete helplessness. Flashbacks of wishing I had done something to try to stop it. Was it because I thought I was weird, different, crazy? Was it because I thought I would be disowned by peers and family? Why am I feeling this way? Why did this happen to me? Why did God allow this to happen? With all of the confusion and questions going on in my head and convinced I was going to be made fun of by everyone who found out, I decided not to say anything to anyone. I decided to hide it deep down, way down, and over time try to convince myself that the event had never happened. To try to convince myself that it would never happen again. To try to convince myself that I'm not some weird kid, and there's nothing wrong with me. This was the beginning of it all.

CHAPTER 3

Aftermath

"Momma tell your children
not to do what I've done..."
—The Animals

I can remember the day after this tragic event like it was yesterday. A sense of fear ran through my body, and it felt like it had complete control over me. I felt scared, really scared. I assume it was a type of defense mechanism, but I can recall immediately trying to convince myself that it was a bad dream and contemplating whether it really did happen. Next, I can remember thinking of possibly telling someone, but for some reason, and till this day, I don't know why, but every part of my body and soul said, "No!" What would Mom and Dad think of me? What would my friends think of me? If I say something, then everyone will know what happened.

I couldn't bear it. I mean come on, decision making at eight or nine years old isn't too sharp for most kids, right? As I mentioned earlier, I decided to hide it, bury it deep, and hope it faded from my memory. I had no idea what repercussions would follow after that decision.

My parents or other friends and family might have a different opinion, but from the age ten through just to about a few months ago, I lived my life with a chip on my shoulder. Understandable, right? A really big chip. No, wait, not a chip; it felt like the goddamn Grand Tetons on my shoulder. Now this chip, or mountain, or post-traumatic stress/experience, whatever you want to call it, shaped my personality, my actions, my soul, and my world.

Now I realize that other people have gone through their own trials and battles, and I'm not writing this book to measure my life experiences against theirs. I'm just sharing my story and hoping someone else can relate their journey with mine and understand that they aren't alone.

Okay, here we go. A brief list should work just fine. The following things or events happened after "that dark day."

1. Lying became natural. To impress others, get what I wanted, or hide things I did not want others to know.

2. Anger and rage became a regular emotion. From when I was ten to twenty-one, I think many people would describe me as an unhappy, angry person. Scuffles and fights happened regularly. Cheating, lying, and bullying my way through middle school. Kicked off the eighth-grade volleyball team for gambling at school; game was called Acey Deucey, a really fun game, but that's not the point.

3. First introduced to sex, drugs, and alcohol at the age of thirteen.

4. In a drive-by shooting in Santa Clara at thirteen years old. Neighbors thought it might have been fireworks or something like that. Those of us who were outside would say that was a damn gun.

5. The regular use of drugs, alcohol, and sex continued throughout high school.

6. To start my senior year in high school, I decided to make things much more stressful and difficult with a DUI and hit-and-run misdemeanor charge. The decision to drink and drive that night would cost me two totaled cars; one was mine, and the other was the parked car I hit. Thank God I was the only one who was injured in the accident. For a few years the incident

was very foggy, but for some weird reason, as time has passed, I was able to remember much more.

As I open my eyes, everything around me is spinning, my head is killing me, and with blurred vision I notice people gathering near my 1994 Toyota 4 Runner. In a drunken slur I realized that my head was halfway through the windshield. I panicked, and I pulled my head back through the hole in the windshield. I can vividly remember the glass cutting my face and top of my head. As I looked through the partially shattered windshield, I noticed a crowd of people gathering near my car and the parked car I'd just totaled.

I panicked. My first drunken/concussed thought was "I've to get home, right now."

From this point on it's still a little hazy but has become clearer as time has passed. I'm really not sure why that is. As I was backing up my dad's 1994 Toyota 4 Runner, I heard the crowd of people saying things like, "Oh, shit this guy is gonna take off." "Does anyone know whose car this is?"

For the people who know the logistics of San Jose, California, the accident took place on

Meridian Avenue and Foxworthy. As I was getting onto Highway 280 North, my car started to drive like it just got smashed on at a monster truck show. The engine was making noise, the car was pulling to the right big time, and loud screeching noise filled the cabin of the car. My car was in really bad shape, but before I had any sense or soberness kick in to pull over and off the road, I found myself driving up the ramp to get onto Highway 17 South. Partially up the ramp my front right tire blew. It sounded like a cannon being fired. I had lost control of my vehicle and was basically driving on my car's rim on the front right side. My car pulled hard to the right and ran right into the guard rail. Sparks were flying all over the place. Somehow my car made it down the off ramp onto Highway 17 South. My car was undrivable, and I was luckily forced to pull over to the right about a half mile from the Hamilton exit on Highway 17.

I knew I was in some serious trouble, so the only thing I could reasonably think to do was to sober up, right? In a drunken/staggering walk I stumbled into the Shell gas station off Hamilton. I remember thinking "Okay, I can do this. Get a bunch of water, some aspirin, and I should be good to go in about thirty minutes." When I came up to the counter the worker at the cash register was looking at me funny. He didn't say anything, but I can remember a funny vibe from him. I didn't say or do anything. I got my water, but I'm not sure if I got aspirin or any other medicines like that. I went outside, sat on the curb, and started to drink the water I'd just bought. Before I knew it two police cars pulled into the gas station and parked right next to me. I knew I was in some serious shit. My big idea of getting sober and getting home was done; it was done long before I even realized it.

One of the officers got out and said, "Hey there, that wouldn't be your Toyota 4 Runner parked on Highway 17 South before the Hamilton exit, would it?"

"Ummm yes, it is, officer," I replied.

"Okay, well before we go any further, we need to take you to the hospital to get cleaned up. We'll ask you a bunch of questions and start the process there," the same officer stated.

"Why do I need to go to the hospital?" I asked

"Seriously?" replied the officer. "You weren't by chance involved in hitting a parked car off Meridian Avenue, were you?" asked one of the police officers.

"Ummm yes, I was, sir," I mumbled softly.

"Well, your head is bleeding, and it looks like you've a fair amount of glass stuck in your head. The worker inside the gas station called us and said, 'I got a high school kid in the store and he's bleeding from the top of his head. Looks like he needs some help or ambulance.'"

The next thing I can remember was getting the handcuffs put on, which is an experience in itself, and being put into the back of one of the police cars. For good reason, the back of the police car is no comfy Cadillac, and with handcuffs on the only way to sit back there is in an uncomfortable position in pain. But again, I understand why it is that way.

While at the hospital I had the glass removed from my head, and during this process I told the police officers what had happened, or at least what I had remembered at the time.

My dad had arrived at the hospital and was immediately called over to talk to the police officers. After a few minutes my dad came over to where I was at. I couldn't even look him in the eyes.

"Well, you're lucky, Matt. Thank God you didn't hurt nobody else, and the police officers said that this accident under the influence of alcohol will be reported, and you'll eventually have a court date. But since you're still a minor and you suffered an injury to your head, you can come home tonight instead of going to jail," my dad stated.

I can't recall if I replied at all to my dad, too embarrassed, too ashamed, too scared. I thought, just get me home. Just get me home.

7. Between my sophomore and senior year in high school, fights became a regular thing. One-on-one, brawls, "jumping people," didn't matter. By the time I was a senior in high school, I found myself surrounded by ex-convicts, people affiliated with the Hells Angels, and people with multiple chips on their shoulders, and any of these individuals or groups were not afraid to let out their anger and hate onto whoever got in their way. After graduating high school, I had a choice—go to school and continue my baseball career or join Jax and the SOA Club per se. On April 27, 2000, my son Jacob was born, and my decision was much easier to make. The Lord works in mysterious ways, and over time I've learned from others to "turn it over" and get out of God's way.

8. My son was born in the Spring of 2000 and having a child at the age of twenty definitely had its own challenges in itself, but it was a major wakeup call that I needed to make a change and get my life in order. By the time I was 21 years old, I stopped my college baseball career, moved back home to California from Oklahoma City, and got a job as a server at Max's Restaurant in Saratoga, California.

   Many difficult decisions were made, and I know I made mistakes along the way, but I wouldn't change anything at all. Without question being a parent is the most rewarding yet challenging responsibility I've had and most likely will ever do, but it's so worth it. Today my son Jacob is nineteen years old and is a fantastic young man. He was the spark that I needed to begin to change. God is good. God is good

9. On one side of the coin, my twenties were great. I got married to my amazing, beautiful wife, I had my son, and my two daughters Brianna and Kaia were born, I was keeping busy working in emergency medical services as an EMT and paramedic, and I was organizing my ideas of a club baseball program for youth and high school ball players in the Bay Area. Who could complain, right? Well, as Sylvester

Stallone said in Rocky (2006), "Life isn't all sunshine and rainbows." I concur with Rocky on this one, and over time I'd learned the difference between the pain and struggle that sometimes shows up in life and the pain and struggle that is *self-inflicted.*

I just mentioned the term self-inflicted. Well, that was definitely the "other side of the coin." My mid- to late twenties to the first few years of my thirties were full of alcohol, blackouts, episodes of rage, and being drunk in public arrests. It was a time that I learned many things through my dark and painful experiences, a time that I may have had to go through to get where I'm at right now, but it was also a time that I wish I did not have to put my family and friends through.

CHAPTER 4

Rock Bottom

"And you can have it all/my empire of dirt/I
will let you down/I will make you hurt."

—Johnny Cash

I woke up on the morning of Christmas 2010 irritable
and agitated. How unfortunate, I mean waking up on
Christmas pissed off, with a beautiful wife and three
amazing kids. Seems a little off, right? Why, you may be
wondering? Well, I let my negative thoughts and past
experiences get the best of me, for about a week before Christmas. Negative materialistic thoughts like,
"You bum, again you don't have enough money to
buy the gifts you want for your family" and insecure
thoughts like "Keep this shit up, Matt, and your wife will
eventually be looking for something better, and your
kids won't be far behind." Past experience thoughts

like "Tonight would be the perfect night to go find that person who violated me in my childhood. I may just kill the fucker!" INSANITY. Pure insanity was my daily way of thinking, and for an alcoholic who is not in recovery, insanity is not only a way of life, but the insanity also spreads into the ones you love and to anyone else who gets close to you.

How does an alcoholic deal with his/her issues? By drinking early and often, and on this particular Christmas, drinking alcohol started at ten a.m. I can remember getting all of the ingredients for spiked hot apple cider, a family favorite recipe, by the way, for at least a decade and highly recommended.

I can remember my wife asking from the living room, "What cha doing, honey?"

"Making hot apple cider," I replied.

Notice how I didn't mention the spiked, aka rum, part of the cider? I thought I was being smooth and was going to fly under the radar, but my wife knew what the hell I was doing. Ya think she couldn't smell the alcohol on my breath? Or see that Captain Morgan bottle that was now empty next to the crock pot? Many bad decisions, the lies, trying to sneak a drink or drinks in without anyone knowing are just a few examples of what alcoholics try to get away with on a regular basis. This disease not only affects us physically, but mentally as well. And what everyone, not just alcoholics or addicts, need to find a way to accept and understand, either positive or negative, is that our actions, decisions, comments, body language, and more affects those around us, and it's usually the people we love and those we're closest with who will either benefit from the positives or get beaten down constantly from the crazy dramatic experiences and stress that brings along with it.

It's getting close to three p.m. Remember this is now the afternoon on Christmas Day, and it's time to get ready for Christmas dinner at my Aunt Charlotte's house that starts around five p.m. It doesn't take long for me to get ready, and by this time I'm feeling pretty good, which means buzzed, in alcoholic terminology.

I overheard my wife tell my kids, "About ten or fifteen minutes until we're out of here."

That was plenty of time for one more drink before we hit the road. One of the many scary things about an addict or alcoholic is that of the mindset "petal to the metal" or "balls to the walls," and this usually runs its course until you get sick, vomit, black out, or unfortunately something much worse.

The drive over to my aunt's house is still to this day a blur. All I know is my wife, Megan, drove, and we made to my aunt's house with no problems or issue;

unfortunately, in just a short few hours, that was all about to change.

Most of the evening was great. Dinner was delicious, for the most part. The conversations and company were fine. Everything was going fine, but unfortunately that would all change.

The main course for this Christmas dinner was prime rib, and when the prime rib came into the kitchen from the barbecue grill, I was appointed to cut/slice the meat. By no means am I an expert at slicing meats, but I was more than happy to help out. While I was cutting the prime rib, my aunt Ruth, may she rest in peace, was critiquing my technique. During this time of my life, I had a short fuse, and almost anything could set me off, and it didn't help that I was drinking all morning and into this Christmas evening. Eventually I had enough and said, "You know what? You guys fucking cut the meat." Alcoholics not in recovery can be a scary thing, so unpredictable, and at any moment shit can hit the fan, and unfortunately it was about to.

I was so pissed off that I had to leave my aunt's house. I stormed outside trying to calm down, salivating at the feeling of rage running through my veins. If you've ever seen the comic character Bruce Banner transform into the Incredible Hulk, that's exactly how I felt. And to this day I realize I was overreacting and a little sensitive toward Aunt Ruth's comments, but I wasn't really pissed off her. I was pissed at the mother fucker who molested me years earlier, and I got wind that morning that he was in town. Time to pay a visit.

You'll have to bear with me about this evening. The majority of this night is still a little fuzzy, and some things that happened that night became clearer as time went on. I can remember walking up to his front door like a bull seeing the color red, and by the time I reached his front porch, somehow, I felt sober. This is it. I'm finally going to confront this guy. Probably not the best decision, especially since I'm drunk, but at this point, fuck it.

I ring the doorbell and knock on the door for a few minutes, and after nobody answers.

I decided to walk away. Honestly, till this day, I'm really glad he didn't open the door that Christmas evening. It has taken a lot of work and steps, but I've gotten to the point of letting go of that terrible event that happened to me as a young child, and with continuous help from the "man upstairs", I just might be able to forgive the guy who did this to me and to be free from all of it.

From this point on in the evening it's still somewhat of a blur, and most of the things that happened were told to me as time passed.

As I walked back toward my aunt's house, my mind and body were still in fight-or-flight mode, not exactly how

I wanted to feel going back to my aunt's Christmas party. As I got a few houses down from the party, I'd noticed a gentleman standing by his car smoking a joint.

Awesome, I thought, just what I needed to calm me down. We "shot the shit" for a few minutes, and finally I asked if I could take a few hits.

The gentleman replied, "Oh, I'm not too sure you want any of this, Matt."

At the time I honestly didn't care what the stuff was; very dangerous, right? I know some of you can relate.

I said, "You know what, man? Things have been so fucked up lately, especially tonight on Christmas, I don't give two shits."

I guess I was convincing enough, because before I knew it I was puffing on that joint. I couldn't help noticing that the effects were heavy and came very quickly; the taste was also different. It didn't have that earthy chronic taste to it. Cannabis users will know what I mean. Only after a few puffs I was good, "really good," as Nacho Libre would say. But little did I realize that those few puffs on the magic dragon, along with all of the alcohol that I drank throughout the course of the day, was about to kick my ass, along with mountains of guilt and regret.

Once I came back and rejoined the Christmas party, the first person I saw was my wife, Megan. Once we made eye contact, I could tell she knew that Matt was in the danger zone and we should probably get going very soon. I'm not sure how much longer we stayed at my aunt's house from this point on. All I can really remember is the car ride home. As stated earlier I had mountains of guilt and regret. Well, on this night, this is unfortunately where it started.

My wife pulled our car around to the front of the house to pick up my son, Jake; two daughters, Brianna and Kaia; and me. At the time my son was ten years old, Brianna two, and Kaia less than a week away from turning big numero uno. I can remember feelings of being very scared and paranoid, like someone or something was after us, as we drove off. After I was riding in the car for about ten or fifteen minutes, my paranoia became too much for me to handle, and it started to affect my wife and children. I started to act out in anger, physically damaging our car by ripping off the rearview mirror and cracking the mirror on the passenger side door. I soon became verbally abusive, shouting obscure obscenities. Unfortunately, my wife had seen the darkest side of me multiple times. That's what typically happens when you are with an alcoholic for ten years who also has many issues that have never been addressed.

By the grace of the man upstairs, my wife was able to convince me to get out of the car. For some reason I can remember watching them driving away, and I was thinking "Man, what the hell is going on? Son of a bitch, I must have screwed up again."

As I walked back to our house, that paranoid feeling that someone was after me was still there. I can recall going through intermittent periods of walking, jogging, and running back toward our house off Meridian Avenue and Branham in San Jose, California. As I got to our house, my paranoia was at its highest of the evening. I was certain that something bad was going to happen to me. I went to the front door. It was locked. I went scuffling into the backyard to see if any of the doors were open. None of them were. A panic attack was now in full effect, and I started yelling and screaming for someone to let me in.

"Somebody is fucking after me. Please let me in," I can recall yelling over and over for a short period of time.

My attention turned to a couple of voices that were calling my name as they were walking near our house. Without hesitation I walked from our backyard to the front of our house and confronted these two people.

As I came to the front of the house, I can recall the two people/images were both dark and blurry. I had no idea who these people were, and I couldn't tell you their age or sex.

As we approached one another both of them spoke to me, except I could not understand anything they were saying. It was like when the teacher spoke in the show *Charlie Brown*. One of the people put their hand on my shoulder, and apparently, I snapped. I grabbed the person closest to me and pulled them to the ground. I was once taught that if you're in a fight or protecting yourself, if you have them on the ground, do not let them up.

And that's exactly what I tried to do. I tried to keep this random person on the ground. After wrestling around with this person for a few seconds, I realized that this person was indeed a man, and now this man was yelling, "Matt, please stop! Matt, please!"

Moments later water came blasting all over me, like there was a single rain cloud sitting over me. I ripped off my shirt feeling like I was Hulk Hogan, not realizing that I was acting like a crazed maniac.

On comes another blackout. Eventually I come to my senses, and I find myself kneeling in the middle of the street, there was puke everywhere, and I was in handcuffs. The flashing lights from the police cars were piercing. I could hear and see crowds of people standing somewhat close to where I was. I could not actually identify who anyone was. Little did I realize that these crowds of people were my neighbors. Two officers came over to where I was kneeling down.

One officer said, "Well, ya all done? Got to throw up anymore?"

I couldn't tell you whether or not I'd responded, but before I knew it, I was helped to my feet and put in the back of the police car. I recall thinking, "What the fuck happened? What in the hell is going on? God damn it. I feel like I'm going to get sick again."

And that's exactly what had happened, I started puking again. All I can really recall at this point is I kept apologizing over and over again. Maybe it's because I worked for eight years in EMS as an EMT and paramedic, so I totally understood what the worse type of calls were. Patients or people associated with vomit was right at the top of the list.

The officer's voices still sounded like the teacher from *Charlie Brown*, so I had no idea what they were saying or talking about, but I have a good idea what it was something like "Are you fucking kidding me, bro?" or probably "Damn! That shit is fucking disgusting. Rank, man! Roll down the damn windows."

All I know is that I'm in the back of a police car, there's puke all over me, fucking everyone sounds like Charlie

Brown's teacher, and I can't keep my eyes open. Time for another blackout.

As I awake, my whole upper body is throbbing, my head feels like it's about to explode, and the smell is unbearable. It's so disgusting that the only thing comparable is a dead body after days or weeks in the middle of summer in Fresno, California. Unfortunately, I knew exactly where I was. The drunk tank downtown at the police station. How do I know that? If you guessed "Probably because you'd been there before," you're absolutely correct.

A few years back I got arrested in downtown San Jose by some university officers for being drunk in public. That, my friends, is a whole different story in itself. But I can assure you that it's another example of me embarrassing myself, putting others through stress and pain, and solidifying that I indeed have an alcohol-abuse problem.

Surprisingly I was pretty much cleaned up. My dress shirt and jeans covered with vomit were gone and replaced by San Jose Police Department's finest orange inmate uniform. I can remember my mind starting racing in panic. What the hell happened? What did I do? Why am I in jail clothes? If this is the drunk tank, then why am I the only one in here? Oh, man, I must have really screwed up this time. For the next several hours I sat in the same spot, asking myself the same questions over and over again. I had a problem. Actually, I knew

I had several problems. The challenge was I willing to accept it and do something about it.

All I can do now is sit here, battle my thoughts and guilt, and wait.

As mentioned previously, I sat in the drunk tank for several hours. Suddenly I could hear keys opening up the door, and it was the best sound I'd ever heard in my life.

"All right, Cesario. Let's go! Time for you to get out of here!"

As I got up my body felt like I got hit by a car; it almost felt like I needed help walking out of there.

"Go through the first door and pick up your belongings. You'll go through another door and your ride will be waiting for you," the officer said to me.

After I get my belongings, I go through a door that leads to a waiting room. The first person I see is Uncle Frank, former US Marine Corps Uncle Frank. At this moment I knew I must have fucked up pretty bad for Uncle Frank to be here. As we made eye contact my uncle's expression confirmed it. I fucked up again. The problem was I still had no idea what had actually happened. There was a good chance my uncle was about to fill me in.

CHAPTER 5

Choice

"It's not how hard you hit, it's how hard you can get hit and keep moving forward...that's how winning is done."

—Rocky

I honestly don't recall anything that happened from the time I met my uncle in the police station waiting room to arriving at my uncle's car to leave the police station. I remember the car ride home, though, or I should say to my uncle's house.

"Well, holy shit, Matt, how are you feeling, man?" my uncle asked.

"I feel like shit," I replied.

"Do you remember what the hell happened last night, Matt?" my uncle asked.

"A little bit," I replied. "Everything is a little blurry."

"Well, Matt, there's only one way to put it, man, you fucked up. You fucked up big time, bro. Megan wants you out. You need to be away from your kids for a while. You've got a problem, Matt. I care about you and your family, and that's why I'm here to pick you up. I'm here to hopefully help you get the help you need. You'll be staying with me at my house for a little while."

"All right. Damn, what the hell happened last night?" I said.

"What do you remember?" My uncle asked.

"I sort of remember leaving Aunt Charlotte's house last night, and I can remember feeling like someone was after me. Actually, I remember two random people confronting me at my house. I think I got into a fight with one or both of them."

I can still recall the look on my uncle's face. It was very similar to when someone is about to tell something bad, like somebody has died.

"Matt, I don't know any other way to say this, but those two people you're talking about; fuck, Matt, that was your mom and dad!"

Initial pain came on as if someone had kicked me right in my nuts. Then that pain overcame my whole stomach area. "Oh my god! Are you fucking kidding me? Fuck me," was something along the lines of my response. "What the hell actually happened?" I asked.

My uncle replied, "Well when I arrived at your house, San Jose police officers were already there, and you were in handcuffs kneeling in the street. You were in bad shape, not only because you were in handcuffs, but you were puking nonstop. After speaking with Megan, something set you off at your aunt's house, and Megan thought it would be best if you guys left and went home. Apparently, you were acting very paranoid on the way home. You were freaked out that someone was looking at you, following you, or something like that, so I guess you broke off the rearview mirror. You got worse as the drive went on, but luckily Megan was able to get you to get out of the car near Highway 85 and Camden Avenue."

As I'm listening to my uncle unravel another "Matt fucked up again" story, nothing but anger and guilt filled my mind and body. At that moment, if I could have ended it all and taken my own life, I just might have done it.

My uncle kept on with the details "By the time you got to your house, you were acting crazy, man, yelling and screaming that someone was after you. Megan was scared and went into the house. Your folks ended up calling me, so I headed over to see what was going on."

My uncle starts shaking his head in disbelief. "When your parents arrived at your house, you came from the backyard. Your dad said as he approached you, he knew something was wrong. Your dad put his hand on your shoulder, and out of nowhere you tackled him to the ground and started throwing punches at him in a drunken rage. Your mom didn't know what to do, so she grabbed the garden hose and sprayed you, hoping you would stop."

"Fucking A, man, unbelievable. Can it get any worse?" I said.

"Unfortunately, Matt, it can get worse, man," my uncle replied. "You came over to your mom and tried to get the hose out of her hands. During that, you pulled your mom to the ground. She's a little banged up, but will be all right."

At the moment I couldn't imagine I could feel any worse. I took a deep breath while shaking my dead, looked up at my uncle with complete desperation, and asked, "And Megan and the kids?"

"Well, they're all okay. You were acting in a crazed, violent, and panicked manner, so Megan had the wit to lock all the doors and call us for help."

"Why in the hell did she call the damn cops?" I asked.

"Although Megan was scared of this situation, she didn't call police. One of the neighbors did. Here's the thing, Matt. You fucked up, man, and as of right now, it is all over, or at least things are on hold with Megan and the kids. I already have a bag packed for you, and you'll be staying with me at my house for a little while. Tomorrow you will have to opportunity to call and get some help. Where that is going to be, I don't know, but the ball is in your court now. Megan and the kids can't be around that kind of behavior, Matt, and I think you know that. You need a shower, bro, so let's get you to the house to get you situated."

At that very moment, I had hit my rock bottom. WTF is wrong with me? Have I turned into a raging, out-of-control, abusive alcoholic? Have I really put my family through this? Am I crazy? Need medication? God damn, Matt, what have you fucking done now? Anger, rage, depression, and self-pity were flowing through my mind and body. At this moment the first thought of suicide crept into my mind, and unfortunately it wouldn't be the last.

CHAPTER 6

Hope

"Hope is a good thing, may be best of things,
and no good thing ever dies."
—Andy Dufrense

When my uncle and I arrived at his house, he showed me around really quick, then brought me upstairs to show me where my room was.

"Right around the corner is the bathroom where you can shower and clean up. Do you want to get some rest and then eat something after?" my uncle asked.

"Yeah, I'll probably get some sleep after I shower," I responded.

"Okay, I have some errands to do, so I'll come check back with you later," my uncle replied

As soon as my uncle left the house, I took a shower to clean off that godawful drunk tank smell. I can recall walking back to the room I was staying in and feeling like fucking dog shit physically, mentally, and spiritually. I was broken, I was depressed, I was disgusted with myself, and I had hit rock bottom. I wanted to just sit in my room and cry myself onto a huge pile of self-pity, but the pure shock and anger with myself wouldn't allow me to get emotional at this point. I closed all the blinds in the room, turned off the lights, and lay on my bed. As I closed my eyes, my whole body felt like a bus had hit me, and I hoped that when I awoke this would all be a bad dream.

At first all I could hear was a faint knock on the door to my room. A few moments later I could hear a voice, but initially couldn't understand what they were saying.

In a semi-irritated response, I replied "Yeah?"

"Matt, it's Uncle Frank. Can I come in?"

"Oh, yeah, come on in" I replied.

"Well, did you get enough rest?" asked my uncle.

"Oh man, I feel like I could sleep definitely for a few more hours," I replied.

"Wow, that's interesting," stated my uncle.

I glanced at him with a confused look. "What do you mean, Uncle Frank?" I asked.

"Well, Matt, you've been asleep for almost two days now," my uncle stated.

"Wow, seriously?" I replied. I can recall thinking WTH? Almost two days? In the past ten years, it didn't matter how much I had partied, I didn't sleep for more than eight to ten hours.

"I figured you can clean up, then we can go grab a bite to eat and talk a little bit. How does that sound?" asked my uncle.

"Sounds good to me," I replied.

After I got ready we went to grab some dinner at the Outback Steakhouse in Campbell, California. During our meal my uncle and I talked about my options and what I was going to do. We had both agreed that I needed to get some help and that time away from my family was probably the best option.

"So, I guess this drinking thing has been an issue for a little while now?" asked my uncle.

"Yes, it has," I replied as I took in a deep breath.

Okay, apologies, but I must pause here and explain something in a little more detail. As far as I can remember, I have always been the hot-head drinker. You know those drinkers who are always having fun, giggling, laughing all the time? Yeah, that's not me. Maybe it would have been nice if I were, but if that was the case I would die of cirrhosis of the liver by the time I turned fifty years of age; more info on cirrhosis of the liver later. I was the drunk that was one drink away from getting thrown in jail or worse. I was the drunk who showed up to all his finals at WVC slammed, wrote "Fuck You, Asshole" on the last page of my chemistry exam. Drove home on Highway 9 drinking a handle of Captain Morgan with the windows down blasting the song "Triumph" by Wu Tang Clan. I was that drunk and let me say this with absolute clarity: This behavior is not cool or meant to be humorous by any means and is nothing but pain, turmoil, and insanity.

Okay, back on track. Over the next few minutes, I explained to my uncle the progression of my alcoholism. My drinking problem without question started in high school. My alcoholism started to really show itself when my family lived in Clovis, California. During this time of my life things seemed to be quite overwhelming. I was working full time as a paramedic with the local ambulance company, my wife was in graduate school at Fresno State, and we were taking care of my son, Jacob, and my daughter, Brianna. Over time things seemed to be going one hundred miles an hour and balancing all my responsibilities was something I was not good at, and without question still learning today.

There were two situations that I feel really contributed in myself jumping two feet into my alcoholism. The first situation was in 2012, when we were going through our fourth custody dispute with my son's mother. The turmoil and stress were through the roof, our family was in jeopardy, and after each day, I felt like I was losing control. Drinking alcohol at the time seemed to be the only thing that could help—that buzz feeling, those few hours of not thinking about all of the stressors and worries in my life. For those people who really know me, I drank booze with the motto of "just one mo' sip," and that motto caused me and the people around me quite a bit of pain, and for that I'm sorry.

The second situation that I feel has helped contribute to my alcoholism was experiencing PTSD related to the working field of EMS. During this time of my life, I had worked eight years in EMS; three of those eight years working as a paramedic. What was it like working in EMS, you may be contemplating. Well, I haven't experienced any other rush or focus that is like having someone else's life in your hands. Many calls were pretty straightforward; look at your patient and determine how sick they are, control the patient's airway, administer oxygen, and get some baseline vital signs. As a medic there's a good chance you've put this patient into a protocol to follow for treatment. If not, no time to dillydally on the scene; load up the patient and start heading into the hospital. This is how many medical or minor trauma calls were in the world of EMS. As stated just a few moments ago, pretty straightforward if you can treat your patient with the correct protocol.

On the flip side of that coin are the calls that test everything you've trained for as a paramedic. These are the calls where patients' lives are in your hands, and the treatment they receive from the time they are in your hands to the time the patient reaches the ER hospital staff is crucial for the patients' condition and survival. The following are a few examples I had working as a medic:

1. Life-threatening traumas—motorcycle accidents, car ejections, shootings, stabbings, falls from fifty feet or higher, electrocutions, and plenty of other examples

2. The list of medical emergencies can be quite long, but the one type of medical calls that really got my heart rate going was airway compromise in toddlers or infants or any related domestic abuse involving kids. Example of an airway compromise would be a choking or a complete airway obstruction. Out of respect of

my patient, and probably breaking fifty HIPPA laws, I won't discuss the child abuse call I had that eventually helped in making the decision to walk away from EMS. This incident happened more than ten years ago, and I still have occasional dreams about that call to this day.

If you're reading this, I want you to know how sorry I'm that you had to go through what you did. It was also the first time I had a call related to this type of incident, so I apologize if I came off as nervous. One of the challenging aspects of EMS is that there are so many incidents in where we never know what happens to our patients after we drop them off at the hospital. This life can be confusing and at times seem dark. Unfortunately, evil shows up, sometimes when we don't expect it, and there are times we can feel it building up. But on the flip side, it took me a while to really believe there's good in this crazy world we live in. There is love and joy in this world that will literally set your soul on fire, and in doing so, you'll unlock the secret in why God put you on this earth. I hope you were given the opportunity to seek out the joys in life. I hope you are living out nothing less than your biggest hopes and dreams. I hope that you've found comfort and peace. "Love is the heart, and the heart is the entrance." –Asian Born.

The Kaiser Chemical Dependency Recovery Program in Santa Clara was next on tap (A.K.A Rehab), and a few days after the notorious Christmas evening of 2010, I was enrolled into its program. I can remember being very nervous, cautious, and scared driving over to the Kaiser Chemical Dependency Facility. It took a half horseshoe to calm me down during the drive over there. Currently I'm grateful to say that I've kicked that habit as well.

As I enter the facility, everything looked pretty much as I had expected. Security guard at the front door, receptionists waiting to check me in, and a little table with complimentary coffee and tea. I had somehow not noticed it initially, but it had my attention now. There were about twenty or thirty people waiting in the lobby area, and it was a mixture of people who looked and probably felt like I did, and as the saying goes "Tow Up From da Flow Up," translation "Tore up from the floor up," and the rest of the people were either young teens or people I was surprised to see there.

If I haven't already, I apologize if and when I come off as being judgmental; I'm working on it.

After a filling out a bunch of paperwork on past medical history and questionnaires about how fucking crazy we thought we were, or the extent of our drug/alcohol problem, it was time for everyone to move from the waiting area into the designated meeting room. This designated meeting room was where we would meet every morning at eight a.m. for the next thirty days. Little did I know, things were about to get real.

As we all waited in the meeting room to see what happened next, the double doors suddenly opened, and a handful of staff entered the room. For whatever it's worth it's what I'd thought the members of the staff would look like. Why did it matter? It really didn't matter, but it's how my jacked-up mind worked sometimes.

I'm in an uncomfortable situation, feeling completely exposed and vulnerable already, borderline wanting a drink. I need to assess the people and staff to see if I feel safe in this environment. If I don't, unfortunately shit tends to hit the fan. The staff starts to go around and introduce themselves. Most of them give a quick background on their experience in the field. Some share their interest and hobbies.

As I glanced around the room, it was no secret that half of us could give two shits about what they were saying at his point. Nothing personal and no disrespect meant, but at this point most of us were at our rock bottom, so 90 percent of what most people had to say had no impact, meaning, or interest...at least that's how it was for me.

One of the staff members came to the front of the room and said, "Okay, now we are going to go around the room and have each of you introduce yourselves. Please make sure to mention your drug of choice."

I could hear most of us sigh in annoyance.

"Better get used to getting honest and uncomfortable, guys," said a different staff member.

For some reason, this immediately made sense to me. If I wanted this work, I had to go all in. Funny thing is that this particular staff member would become a shining light from the heavens and a huge influence in my recovery from alcoholism.

As we finished introducing ourselves, I had grouped everyone's drug of choice and had guesstimated that most of us were there for alcohol addiction. Next was prescription drugs, followed by crystal meth. There were a few that had marijuana as their drug of choice, but they left the program after the first day, so I am not counting them.

Another staff member came to the front of our group and said, "Okay, now I want all my people who have alcohol as their drug of choice stand up."

More than a dozen of us stood up.

"Based on our statistics, more than half of you will drop out of this program, and most likely more will not be able to stay sober."

All of us start looking at each other anxiously.

"However, if you can put twelve months into this program, your chances of staying sober the following year are almost 90 percent, and if you can complete our eighteen-month program, your chances in putting together multiple years of sobriety skyrockets."

Hearing this for some reason immediately showed a light at the end of the tunnel. It just made sense to me. I thought, do this program, fucking gut it out, and you'll get your life and family back. Don't be stupid, Matt. The answer is right here.

And away we go. The next thirty days would challenge me like nothing had before. From eight a.m. to three p.m. was for the chemical-dependency program. During our chemical-dependency program, we all went to AA meetings across town from noon to one p.m. One of the requirements of the program was everyone had to attend another AA meeting of our choice, along with the meeting we attended at lunch during the program. For most people in the program, a night meeting was part of their routine. A few of us went to meetings before the program started at eight a.m., and for the next two years, five to seven days out of the week, that ended up being my morning routine.

Many days of the program were quite intense. You've heard of the saying "You get out of it what you put in." Well, this was definitely the case in regard to finding your place in recovery, and the key to this place of serenity was honesty. We were told this on many occasions by our counselors and doctors at the recovery program, and this was also echoed throughout the walls of AA.

I had hit my rock bottom, and I was committed to doing whatever it took not to lose my family. If this recovery thing took looking at myself in the mirror, being completely fucking honest about everything, no sugar-coating shit, well then, I was in. Yes, I was scared, yes, I was doubtful, and yes, fear ran through my entire body, but I felt like I had no other options. The only other option was to fucking die, and thank the lord, I wasn't quite there yet.

As time went on, I became to realize that this honesty thing was working. Was it challenging, difficult, emotional, and sometimes close to confrontational? Absolutely it was, but every time I overcame an obstacle or confronted an issue head on, I started to see the light at the end of the tunnel. I started to see the recovery and AA program working. I started to feel that maybe there was hope after all. Most importantly, I started to hear and feel God speaking to me again.

Before I knew it, I was on my way to celebrating thirty, sixty, and ninety days of sobriety. The recovery program and AA were working simultaneously, and I was back home with my family. Things were actually looking pretty good. I was committed to finishing the whole eighteen-month recovery program, and I was getting through the steps of AA. I can remember thinking to myself, "If I can just keep doing this and stay committed, what could go wrong?" Well, at this point I think you can see how these things go in my life, and unfortunately, the next several years not only didn't really go how I planned, but also didn't go how my family thought things were going to turn out.

CHAPTER 7

Struggles

"Ay yo, I'm slippin, I'm falling. I can't get up.
Get me back on my feet so I can tear shit up."
–DMX

All right, I'm going to fast forward a little bit, and I can assure you that things will get better, and if you've stuck with me through this point of the book, maybe you can go a little bit further.

At this point in my life, I had a few years of sobriety in the tally column, I graduated from the eighteen-month CPRP Recovery Program, and I was sponsoring a few people that were also in recovery. I also decided to go back to school, so I enrolled in a few classes at SJSU. From the outside things probably looked some-what okay, but they weren't. For some reason I still felt broken inside. I still felt the presence of some sort of evil or turmoil. For a period of time, I felt I tried my best to keep these feelings from affecting my family, but in time they did. Unfortunately, sobriety wasn't going to cure all my problems.

My PTSD and anxiety were at times out of control. I can remember being up and down, moody all the time, and it wasn't like I was starving. I put on almost forty pounds since going into recovery. Unfortunately, when things got too stressful, anger and rage would take over and fuck everything up again. It felt like there was a dark cloud that followed me everywhere I went, that there was some sort of evil presence that was daily trying to control my mind, body, and soul. This evil presence was smart, cunning, and patient, and I know some of you can relate to what I'm saying. I was like Bruce Banner and the Hulk from the Marvel Movies, calm, cool, and collected one moment, and then within a blink of an eye I turned into this raging monster. There were so many times I would cry to my wife out of frustration on why I acted like this. Why in the fuck was I like this? How in the hell could I treat my family like this? Am I a fucking psychopath?

It eventually got to the point in where thoughts and comments were made about death and suicide. I would go through these periods on and off, and unfortunately, they would last for nine years into my recovery.

I can't go any further until I address and apologize to my wife and kids. When I look back at this time in our lives and in my recovery, there are so many things I wish I could have done differently. So many times, I wish I would have made a different decision, comment, or action. I know I've caused pain in all of your lives, I'm so sorry. In different ways, most I cannot explain, I believe that God and the universe balance things out, along with the karma I had created in my life up to this point. All of you are the best things in my life, and I will always be here for you, love you, and fight for you whenever necessary. I'm sorry, so sorry. I pray you'll find it in your heart forgive me in time.

CHAPTER 8

The Day That Changed My Life and My Perspective

> "Yesterday is history, tomorrow is a mystery, but today is a gift. That is why it is called present."
> —Master Oogwy

The day was September 14, 2019, and it was a big day for my beautiful wife, Megan. She was being recognized in multiple areas from her health and wellness business and earning an incentive trip to Mexico that we would take in February 2020. I would say things leading up to this event were as usual, shitbag crazy and stressful.

Hail Mary, full of grace, the Lord is with thee; blessed art thou among women and blessed is the fruit of thy womb. Jesus, Holy Mary, mother of God, pray for us sinners now, and at the hour of our death. Amen.

God, please forgive me for what I've put my kids through. Son of a bitch, it sucks. Fucking sucks. You can't turn back the clock; you can't go back in time. You can't take back the scars you create. Fucking sucks. Be better than me. Please learn from my mistakes and shortcomings better than I did.

Besides the bullshit I was creating, I was personally and physically feeling like death. Seriously, I thought parts of me inside were fucking dying, especially in my head. There were seven days of headaches and pain lead-ing up to this day, but my stubborn ass wouldn't go get checked out, and today was an important day for Megan. It meant a lot to me to be there for her. After a long 420 session I headed down to Sacramento to meet my wife at the event. I had a panic attack trying to find parking downtown by the event, so things were not off to a good start. As I was walking toward the event building, I kept having intermittent periods of a sharp pain in the middle of my head, and it would last anywhere from three to ten seconds. Finally, I arrived at the event and met up with Megan, and right away I could tell she knew something wasn't right.

"Are you okay?" asked Megan

"No, not really, but I'll be okay, babe. All good," I replied.

"Well, if you need to go, no problem. Take care of your-self. I've got to go. I'll have my phone on me. Love you," my wife said as she walked toward the event building.

Over the next hour I would meet up with various team members in my wife's business. As we found our seats in the auditorium, I was surprised at how many people were there, probably around seven hundred to eight hundred people. As the event got under way, I started to feel a sharp pain in the center of my head. On the pain scale that most of us our aware of, I would say it was around a five out of ten at this point.

Music started playing. Everyone started cheering and jumping around. Over the next twenty minutes the pain in my head would go from a five to about an eight, and I had a ringing sensation in my head and was very sensitive to light and sound. I really didn't feel well, and I knew that I had to get home. I leaned over to one of our friends and said, "Hey, I fucking feel like shit. I have to get home. I'll send Meg a text."

She gave me a hug and said, "Hope you feel better, and drive home safely."

I looked back and nodded as I headed for the exit.

As I walked outside the auditorium, I couldn't remember where I had parked. I immediately started feeling anxious, and luckily I had noticed a building across the street that I'd walked by when arriving at the event, so I started to walk that way, and it seemed like I had been walking in the same direction for at least a half a dozen blocks and I was sweating bullets due to the central California heat. While I was walking, I recalled that I parked in a parking lot building, so I just had to find it by the grace of God and with some lucky charms.

I'm not certain, but I guess after about another half dozen blocks or so, I recognized the parking building my car was in. I headed up a few flights of stairs, paid my parking ticket fee, got in my car, and started to head back home to Folsom. Depending on traffic, and which part of Sacramento you're coming from, to Folsom it was usually about thirty minutes.

As I was driving through downtown Sacramento, the pain in my head was increasing. I started to feel nauseated, and overall, I really felt like shit. Finally, I stopped at the intersection where I could get onto the freeway. After a few seconds I felt really sick, and suddenly I fucking projectile vomited all over myself and the damn steering wheel. I think I threw up two or three times. As I try to find something to clean myself with, I glanced over to my left, and there was a couple in their car looking at me in shock, like they were waiting for my fucking head to start spinning around like from the movie *The Exorcist*.

Of course, the damn light turns green, and away we go. As I'm driving onto Highway 50 W, I'm cursing like Joe Pesci from the movie *Goodfellas*. I can't exactly remember what I grabbed, but I found something to somewhat clean myself and part of the steering wheel. "Oh, you got to be mother fucking kidding me," I can remember saying out loud. I had to throw up again. As I'm driving down Highway 50, I'm looking for something, please, anything, to vomit in. I felt like Jeff Daniels in the bathroom scene from the movie *Dumb and Dumber*, except my stuff was coming out the opposite way. Freaking disgusting, I know, and I apologize. As I reach behind my seat, lo and behold I pull out a full box of Kleenex. Under the circumstances I would say I get a pass on the next decision I made. For some reason I'd decided to take out all the Kleenex out of the box. I felt sick and there was nothing I could do, I threw up in the empty Kleenex box, and you can guess the godawful nasty mess it made...and the smell...oh, the smell would make a maggot gag.

"Oh Lord have mercy," I can remember shouting out loud. Then I felt it was time for some more Joe Pesci impersonations. However luckily, I had a sense of relief because I recognized the last exit I had just passed on the freeway, and a sigh of relief hit me, because I knew I was almost home.

This is what I remember when luckily arriving safely at home. I don't remember parking the car, opening the door to our home, or even seeing our dog, Kale. I can recall feeling like I had a fever, and the pain in my head was definitely still there. I decided to take a cold shower, hoping that it would bring my fever down. I can't remember getting out of the shower, but I can recall making it to our bed and falling on it like a ton of bricks. Lights out.

Over the next two days my condition would stay the same, and at times it appeared to have worsened. I was pretty much bed bound, and I had hardly any type of appetite. My stubbornness took over, and I refused my beautiful wife's advice and would not go to the hospital. Having said that, I would have no choice come Monday evening. I kept having feelings of fever, so I kept taking cold showers on and off, hoping they would help.

This time things didn't go so smoothly or as planned. All I can really remember is waking up on the bathroom floor, and Megan was calling my name. She has mentioned to me that when I got my conscience back, when I looked at her, my eyes were pinpointed, and I had a gaze or look on my face like when a fighter gets knocked out or when Deebo knocked out Red in the movie *Friday*. Anyhow, here I am, lying on the floor, dead weight. That's five feet, eight inches tall and all of at least 225 at this time, and this 225 is more like the ice cream Thor character from the *Avengers End Game* movie. Basically, there's no way Megs is getting me up off the floor. My legs were slipping underneath me, but somehow, with her medical knowledge, she was able to help get me back to bed. What's next? That is right, call 911 and get the fire crew and ambulance here to help.

My wife is such a trooper. While the ambulance was on its way to our house, Meg was able to dry me off and somehow get me into some clothes before the crew got here. I could hear the fire truck and ambulance sirens as they were both around the corner from our house. It was the evening and both of my daughters had gone to bed but were awakened by all the ruckus. When the fire crew arrived, I noticed the look of concern on my daughters' faces. I grabbed my wife's hand and said, "What the hell is going on? Am I fucking dying or what?"

Megan looked at me and replied, "Just relax and breathe, babe. The ambulance will be here soon."

As the fire crew came into our bedroom, I can recall being relived I had some clothes on. That would have sucked to be "too buck Chuck" on the floor in front of a bunch of dudes, right?

The fire crew came in, asked a few questions, and in no time had me secured in a transfer seat to take me downstairs and out to the ambulance. The ride in the ambulance to the hospital was about what I thought: some oxygen, heart monitor, and an IV just in case some meds needed to be administered en route or at the hospital.

Once we arrived at the hospital, I was brought to a room and was told that once my wife arrived, they'd direct her to this room, and that the doctor would be in shortly to see me.

It didn't take long for the ER doctor to come into the room I was in. He was a young doctor, not like it matters, right? Well, actually maybe it does. We all like someone with some experience and a little time under their belt, right? Especially when it comes to your health.

The doctor ran multiple tests and other than some elevated white blood cells, he told us he couldn't find the cause of the headache. He was just going to treat the headache and plan to send me home. As I was just lying in the bed in pain, my wife explained my symptoms and situation to the doctor, and when the doctor heard my her say that this had been going on for more than ten days, the doctor looked over at me and said, "Ten days? Really? Okay, well, that changes things. We need to scan the head right away."

The "Oh shit" factor just set in. I looked at my wife with concern.

She looked at me and said, "They need to rule out a possible tumor."

Duck on a pond? Yeah, that was definitely me, but at this point, I was in so much pain that I was pretty much game for anything to figure out what the hell was going on.

"Okay, sounds good, doc," I replied.

My wife and I sat in the room nervously waiting for me to be taken for a CT scan. I can recall looking at Megan and asking her, "Am I dying? Because it fucking feels that way." I started to get emotional out of fear and frustration.

My beautiful wife did what she was so good at, comforting and just being there for me.

Suddenly a knock was at the door and there was a nurse to take me for the CT scan. Too bad CT scans don't give MRI-type imaging, because that is the way to go, especially if you experience any type of anxiety or claustrophobia. About fifteen minutes later, I was finished with the scan and back in the ER room with Meg.

The nurse glanced back and mentioned, "The doctor will go over your CT scan and come back to discuss the results once he is finished. Try to get some rest."

Rest? Yes, absolutely, we both needed some rest right about then.

I believe that my wife and I got about thirty to sixty minutes of rest before the ER doctor came back to our room. "Sorry to wake you guys, but the CT scan results are back..." There was a slight pause from the doctor. "Well, I'm not going to beat round the bush here. Matt, you have a tumor in your brain, and actually it's about the size of a golf ball."

I glanced at my wife as she grabbed hold of my hand. Both of us took a deep breath.

The ER doctor continued to share information about our situation. "Chances are this tumor has been going on for a while, but we won't actually know for sure until you get an MRI. How are you doing, Matt?"

I took another deep breath and looked up at the doctor and replied, "I'm kind of in shock really." I sarcastically chuckled. "What are my options?" I asked.

The doctor, in a calm manner, got comfortable and explained the situation. "Well, you really have only two. The first is you do nothing and pretty much see what happens. You know, you could live up in the mountains and see how it goes, but eventually, this tumor will take your life, Matt; exactly when is anyone's guess. You're experiencing quite bit of pain and symptoms right now, so it could be sooner rather than later. Option two is getting you to our hospital in Sacramento and prepping you for surgery. I have already spoken to the on-call neurosurgeon at the Kaiser hospital in Sacramento. The first step would be to get you an MRI. The MRI imaging produces much clearer imaging than CT scans. If that's something you decide to do, then we need to get that process started."

On one side of the coin I remember thinking okay, what the hell is going on here? Please fucking tell me I'm dreaming right now. Okay, good one, fucking joke is over, but on the other side of the coin I felt a sense of calmness, acceptance, and serenity. It was almost like it all finally came together and started to make sense to me.

By this point in the book, I think we can agree I'm two steps away from full on bat-shit crazy, but in all serious-ness, I felt like I finally understood what the pain was, the feeling of a dark demon in my head, the feeling of not having control, the feeling of dying slowly.

"I believe that true focus lies somewhere between rage and serenity." –Professor Charles Xavier

And I would say that this is similar to finding the path and life of acceptance and inner peace.

CHAPTER 9

Saved

"I knew a man who once said, 'Death smiles at us all. All a man can do is smile back.'"
—Maximus Dessimus Merridius

Well, if you've stuck with me up to this point, first off, thank you for your support and interest. Second, you're almost at the finish line. This is the last chapter in this nonfiction tale.

All right, after speaking with the neurosurgeon at Kaiser hospital in Sacramento, we agreed that I would have surgery to remove the tumor in my brain on the morning of September 18, 2019.

I can't recall much between leaving the ER in Roseville to being wheeled down to the operating room for surgery except family visiting and the feeling that this could be it. Being pushed in a hospital gurney on your way down to have brain surgery is pretty fucking surreal. The cool and calming thing was the surgery tech guy who was taking me to surgery was awesome, funny, and easy to talk to.

As we reached the floor where the operating room was located and as the elevator doors opened, I could see the hospital waiting room. The first people I saw, of course, were my beautiful wife, Megan; my parents; and a handful of other family members. Words can't express how grateful and lucky I'm in having family like I do, especially at that particular moment. Seeing everyone for a brief moment made me feel comforted and reassured me that I was making the right decision in having this procedure.

As we entered the hallway leading to the operating room, I put the "golden light of protection" around me and my family members in the waiting room. I can recall thinking, "All right, God, I'm going to leave this up to you and the doctors."

We entered the OR, and I saw at least ten or fifteen people waiting for me by the operating table, and maybe close to a dozen other doctors waiting to learn from this medical procedure, possibly in their internship.

As soon as the hospital gurney was at the side of the OR table, it seemed like everyone had something to do. One person started talking to me and asking a few simple questions. A gentleman came to the side of me and said, "Matt, we're going to start giving you anesthesia, okay? Just relax and breath normally."

"All right," I responded.

A breathing mask was placed over my face. A few moments later I heard a voice say,

"Okay, Matt, go ahead and start counting down from one hundred."

I might have made it to somewhere in the low nineties, but I was out pretty quickly. "Say goodnight, Irene."

As I slowly opened my eyes, I heard a faint voice in the background. I couldn't really make out who it was or where the sound was coming from. Immediately I felt pain and soreness throughout my head, but it wasn't too overwhelming, because I could still feel the effects of the medications and anesthesia from surgery. From this point until the following morning, I couldn't tell you what happened. Well, there was one thing that eventually had to happen, right? If you guessed bowel movement, come on down and claim your prize. Taking a fucking shit post brain surgery in a god damned bed pan the size of a Tupperware dish is the closest damn thing to childbirth I'll ever come to. I know it still comes nothing close to what women experience in labor, but my god, was that experience traumatic in itself.

Okay, lets rewind a little bit really quick, and let me add in a few minor details that y'all should know:

1. At some point between waking up post-surgery and the morning, I had spoken to a few of the neurosurgeons and they explained that the surgery had went well, but unfortunately as of right then, I had no function on my left side.

2. When you have surgery, you receive the VIP treatment with a top-notch A1000 Foley fucking catheter, which is another god damn book in itself.

3. Apparently I was pretty agitated and took my frustrations out on some of the hospital staff members in ICU. Again, I apologize to all of the hospital staff members I gave a hard time to; a few f-bombs might have been dropped.

All right, so it's now sometime in the morning, the day after my surgery, and I have to go *numero dos*. I quickly hit the Call button, and shortly after, a nurse replies, "Hello, can I help you?"

I replied, "Ummm, yeah, hi. I need to ummm go to the bathroom."

The nurse replied, "Oh just go ahead, sir, you have a Foley catheter in."

"Umm…"

That's all I was able to say before the nurse said, "Oh, you need to have a bowel movement. Okay, someone will be right in."

As I'm lying in the hospital bed waiting for some assistance, I find myself getting anxious and diaphoretic. Suddenly the curtain around my bed opens and two nurses—one male and one female—enter somewhat cautiously. God damn, I would too.

"All right, Matt, first bowel movement post brain surgery is a good sign," one of the nurses states.

I can remember thinking something along the lines of "Yippee-ki-yay, MF." –John McClane.

So, I've decided not to go any further in detail about my first and hopefully last bed pan experience. Having said that, I'll relate my experience to actor and comedian Martin Lawrence in his stand-up show *Runteldat*. If you've already seen it, then you can understand what I'm talking about, and I'm also laughing along with you, and that's where I'll leave this reminiscence.

The first few days after surgery were really tough. I was very agitated, had no appetite, and as mentioned earlier, I had no function on my left side, which the staff explained can happen with this type of surgery, but usually function comes back within a few days. I was going on day five. My head felt like it had gone a few seconds with Iron Mike, and it looked like I just escaped a few hours of torture from the *Texas Chainsaw Massacre*. I was definitely not a good patient for the first few days. For those who knew my incredible Grandma Viola Cesario, you can say I channeled her a few times during those first few days. Some would believe that her spirit was there with me in my hospital room, and when she felt like it, her spirit would jump into my body, kind of like from the movie *Ghost* with Demi Moore, and I would yell out at a nurse, "Hey, god damn it!" or to a few male nurses I'd say something like, "Hey, thanks a lot, asshole."

I'm laughing along, but in all seriousness, my Grandma Vi was something else. I can probably write a whole book by sharing her story as well…light bulb! But sometimes I really didn't know reality or if I was hallucinating or something like it, especially the first few days.

When my mental state started to become more stable, my appetite started to slowly come back, and the food was actually pretty good. Quick shout out to the culinary service down at Sacramento Kaiser; that beef stroganoff was the bomb. There was a weekly farmers market at the hospital, where Kaiser got its fresh fruit. Fruit bowls were a must at every meal, and I quickly became obsessed with oranges. Seriously, one of the best things I've ever tasted in my life was an orange Creamsicle lollipop two pills deep, if you know what I mean. Again, nothing but honesty here, and like I said earlier,

"Momma, tell your children not to do what I've done."
—The Animals

The life of an addict's mind—the struggles, the ups, the downs, the balance…God.

Getting my appetite back and looking forward to meals was something positive I really needed but getting the use of my left side again was the turning point when I felt that things were going to be okay.

For a few days, though, I was like Beatrice Kiddo from the movie *Kill Bill Volume 2*, lying in the back of the Pussy Wagon looking at my feet and saying, "Wiggle your big toe," all while watching *Hunger Games* for the hundredth time. But it didn't matter what obstacles I was facing in the hospital. Whether it was learning how to walk again, having my god damn Foley catheter changed while I was awake, lying in my hospital bed half naked with fucking drool running down my face while trying to locate the god damn Call button so I could take what the RN staff called a "poopie" in what felt like a fucking two-by-two Tupperware bowl, or being claustrophobic and taking multiple MRIs, feeling like I was literally being buried alive—none of that mattered once I saw my amazing wife walking down the hall toward my room door.

Lying in the hospital bed feeling totally helpless, when I saw her, time seemed to low down, my perspective started to become more optimistic, I felt so lucky to be alive, and I felt so blessed and grateful to have my beautiful wife by my side. At times I would find myself just looking at her. My mind would race through all of the crazy, fun things we had done over the years, how this fucking amazing woman decided to be with me through the good and bad times. My wife is the best; that's as simple as I can put it, and I can't wait to have a front-row seat in watching her change the world.

Before I knew it, I was being transferred from the ICU to a lower "patient risk" area of the hospital. It was there I was told that if things continued to progress well, I would be able to be discharged and go home within the next few days. You can imagine how happy I was to hear of that possibility.

It was at this point in my life that I finally heard it. I could finally hear Him. Okay, God, I'm listening. Apparently, it's not my time yet. There must be more things to see, people to meet, and people to help; more giving back to others, lifting one another up, listening to others, telling others to love one another and to pass it on to someone else who needs it. You must have more work for me to do. Thank you for saving me so I could continue with the life you've given me and give back to those in similar situations.

Transformation begins now.

"My mission in life is not merely to survive, but to thrive, and to do so with some passion, some compassion, some humor, and some style"
—Maya Angelou